Programming

Q&A

500+

Computer and Programming Q&A

Sharif Ahmed

Title: "500+ Computer and Programming Q&A"

Unlock the programming and computer science world with "500+ Computer and Programming Q&A" by Sharif Ahmed. This comprehensive book is your ultimate guide to unraveling the intricacies of programming, computer science, and data science. With over 500 meticulously curated questions and concise answers, you'll explore various topics and find solutions to most of the interview and viva questions in these fields.

Start your transformative learning journey today. Get your copy and take the first step toward mastering programming, computer science, and data science.

1.   **What is a programming language?**

Answer: A programming language is a formal language that is used to write instructions that can be executed by a computer to perform a specific task.

2.   **What is a variable in programming?**

Answer: A variable is a named storage location in a program's memory used to hold data that can be changed during program execution.

3.   **What is a data type?**

Answer: A data type defines the type of data a variable can hold, such as integers, floating-point numbers, characters, and more.

4.   **How do you declare a variable in Python?**

Answer: In Python, you can declare a variable like this: **variable_name = value**.

5.   **What is a comment in programming?**

Answer: A comment is a text in the code that is not executed but used for documentation and explanations. In Python, you can use # for single-line comments and '" or """ for multi-line comments.

6.   **What is a loop in programming?**

Answer: A loop is a control structure that allows a set of instructions to be executed repeatedly as long as a certain condition is met.

7. **What is an if statement in programming?**

Answer: An if statement is a control structure that allows you to execute a block of code if a specified condition is true.

8. **What is a function in programming?**

Answer: A function is a block of code that performs a specific task and can be reused throughout a program.

9. **What is debugging in programming?**

Answer: Debugging is the process of identifying and fixing errors (bugs) in a program to ensure it works correctly.

10. **What is an IDE (Integrated Development Environment)?**

Answer: An IDE is a software application that provides tools for writing, testing, and debugging code, typically including a code editor, compiler, and debugger.

11. **What is a compiler?**

Answer: A compiler is a program that translates source code into machine code or another form that can be executed directly by a computer.

12. **What is a string in programming?**

Answer: A string is a data type representing a sequence of characters, such as text. In Python, strings are typically enclosed in single or double quotes.

13. **What is an array in programming?**

Answer: An array is a data structure that can hold multiple values of the same data type. It allows you to access elements by their position (index) in the array.

14. **What is a for loop?**

Answer: A for loop is a control structure that iterates over a range of values or elements, executing a block of code for each iteration.

15. **What is a while loop?**

Answer: A while loop is a control structure that repeatedly executes a block of code as long as a specified condition is true.

16. **What is an object in programming?**

Answer: An object is an instance of a class in object-oriented programming. It encapsulates data and behavior related to a specific entity.

17. **What is a class in programming?**

Answer: A class is a blueprint or template for creating objects. It defines the attributes and methods that objects of that class will have.

18. **What is inheritance in OOP?**

Answer: Inheritance is a mechanism in object-oriented programming where a new class (subclass or derived class) can inherit properties and methods from an existing class (base class or parent class).

19. What is a constructor in OOP?

Answer: A constructor is a unique method in a class that is automatically called when an object of the class is created. It is used to initialize the object's attributes.

20. What is encapsulation in OOP?

Answer: Encapsulation is the concept of bundling the data (attributes) and methods (functions) that operate on the data into a single unit, called a class.

21. What is polymorphism in OOP?

Answer: Polymorphism is the ability of objects of different classes to respond to the same method in a way that is specific to their individual classes. It allows for method overriding.

22. What is a parameter in a function?

Answer: A parameter is a variable in a function that receives a value when the function is called. It is used to pass data to the function.

23. What is a return statement in a function?

Answer: A return statement is used to send a value back from a function to the code that called it. It marks the end of the function's execution.

24. What is a method in Java?

Answer: In Java, a method is a block of code that performs a specific task and is defined within a class.

25. What is the main method in Java?

Answer: The **main** method in Java is the entry point for a Java program. It is where the program begins its execution.

26. What is the difference between "==" and ".equals()" in Java for comparing strings?

Answer: In Java, "==" compares references for objects, while **.equals()** compares the actual content (characters) of strings.

27. What is a package in Java?

Answer: A package in Java is a way to organize related classes and interfaces into a single unit. It helps in preventing naming conflicts and provides modularity.

28. What is a Java interface?

Answer: An interface in Java is a collection of abstract methods (methods without a body) that must be implemented by any class that claims to implement that interface.

29. What is a Java exception?

Answer: An exception in Java is an event that occurs during the execution of a program and disrupts the normal flow of instructions. Exception handling is used to deal with these events.

30. What is a try-catch block in Java?

Answer: A try-catch block is used to catch and handle exceptions in Java. The code that may throw an exception is placed within the **try** block, and the corresponding exception-handling code is placed in the **catch** block.

31.   **What is a null pointer exception in Java?**

Answer: A null pointer exception occurs when you try to access or call a method on an object that is **null** (not initialized).

32.   **What is the Java Virtual Machine (JVM)?**

Answer: The JVM is an integral part of the Java platform that interprets Java bytecode and executes Java applications.

33.   **What is the difference between an interpreter and a compiler?**

Answer: An interpreter translates code one line at a time and executes it, while a compiler translates the entire code into machine code before execution.

34.   **What is a version control system (VCS)?**

Answer: A version control system is a software tool that helps manage changes to source code over time, facilitating collaboration and tracking of code history.

35.   **What is Git, and how is it used?**

Answer: Git is a distributed version control system used to track changes in source code. It allows multiple developers to work on the same project and merge their changes.

36. **What is an array in JavaScript?**

Answer: An array in JavaScript is a data structure that stores multiple values in a single variable. It is indexed and ordered.

37. **What is a function in JavaScript?**

Answer: A function in JavaScript is a block of reusable code that can be called to perform a specific task.

38. **What is the document.getElementById function in JavaScript?**

Answer: The **document.getElementById** function is used to retrieve an HTML element on a web page by its unique **id** attribute.

39. **What is a callback function in JavaScript?**

Answer: A callback function is a function that is passed as an argument to another function and is executed after the completion of the outer function.

40. **What is the difference between null and undefined in JavaScript?**

Answer: null is an assignment value that represents the absence of a value, while **undefined** means a variable has been declared but has not been assigned a value.

41. **What is a loop in JavaScript?**

Answer: A loop in JavaScript is a control structure that allows a set of statements to be executed repeatedly as long as a specified condition is true.

42. **What is an object in JavaScript?**

Answer: An object in JavaScript is a collection of key-value pairs, where each key is a string (or symbol) and each value can be any data type.

43. **What is an event listener in JavaScript?**

Answer: An event listener is a function that waits for a specific event to occur and then performs an action in response to that event, such as clicking a button.

44. **What is the purpose of the console.log function in JavaScript?**

Answer: The **console.log** function is used for debugging and to display messages or values in the browser's developer console.

45. **What is the difference between let, const, and var in JavaScript for variable declaration?**

Answer: let and **const** are block-scoped, and **const** variables cannot be reassigned. **var** is function-scoped and can be reassigned.

46.   What is a JSON object in JavaScript?

Answer: A JSON object is a lightweight data interchange format in JavaScript that represents data as key-value pairs. It stands for JavaScript Object Notation.

47.   What is a package manager in programming?

Answer: A package manager is a tool that automates the process of installing, updating, and managing external libraries or packages used in a project.

48.   What is an API (Application Programming Interface)?

Answer: An API is a set of rules and protocols that allows different software applications to communicate and interact with each other.

49.   What is a web API?

Answer: A web API is an API that is accessible over the internet, allowing applications to request and exchange data with web servers.

50.   What is a SQL database?

Answer: A SQL database is a type of relational database management system (RDBMS) that uses structured query language (SQL) for managing and querying data.

51.   What is a primary key in a database table?

52.   **Answer:** A primary key is a column or a set of columns in a database table that uniquely identifies each row. It ensures data integrity and enforces uniqueness.

53.   **What is a foreign key in a database table?**

Answer: A foreign key is a column in a database table that establishes a link between the data in two tables. It enforces referential integrity.

54.   **What is a SQL SELECT statement?**

Answer: A SQL SELECT statement is used to retrieve data from a database table. It specifies which columns to retrieve and may include conditions for filtering.

55.   **What is an SQL JOIN statement?**

Answer: An SQL JOIN statement is used to combine rows from two or more tables based on a related column between them.

56.   **What is a software framework?**

Answer: A software framework is a pre-built foundation that provides a structure for building software applications. It includes reusable components and libraries.

57.   **What is versioning in software development?**

Answer: Versioning is the practice of assigning unique identifiers (versions) to software releases or code changes to track and manage changes over time.

58.   **What is agile software development?**

Answer: Agile is an iterative and flexible approach to software development that emphasizes collaboration, customer feedback, and delivering working software in short cycles.

59.   **What is a software bug?**

Answer: A software bug is an error, flaw, or unexpected behavior in a program that causes it to produce incorrect or unexpected results.

60.   **What is the role of a software tester?**

Answer: A software tester is responsible for identifying and reporting bugs, ensuring that software meets quality standards, and verifying that it works as intended.

61.   **What is source code control?**

Answer: Source code control (or version control) is the practice of managing and tracking changes to source code, allowing multiple developers to work on the same project.

62.   **What is a data structure in programming?**

Answer: A data structure is a way of organizing and storing data to perform operations efficiently. Examples include arrays, linked lists, and trees.

63.   **What is a stack data structure?**

Answer: A stack is a linear data structure that follows the Last-In, First-Out (LIFO) principle, where the most recently added item is the first to be removed.

64. **What is a queue data structure?**

Answer: A queue is a linear data structure that follows the First-In, First-Out (FIFO) principle, where the first item added is the first to be removed.

65. **What is a linked list data structure?**

Answer: A linked list is a data structure that consists of a sequence of elements, each of which points to the next element. It is often used for dynamic data storage.

66. **What is a binary tree data structure?**

Answer: A binary tree is a hierarchical data structure in which each node has at most two children, a left child and a right child.

67. **What is recursion in programming?**

Answer: Recursion is a technique where a function calls itself to solve a problem, often breaking the problem down into smaller, similar subproblems.

68. **What is a pointer in programming?**

Answer: A pointer is a variable that stores the memory address of another variable. It is used for direct memory manipulation and efficient data access.

69.   **What is a software design pattern?**

Answer: A software design pattern is a general, reusable solution to a common problem in software design. It provides a blueprint for structuring code.

70.   **What is the Model-View-Controller (MVC) design pattern?**

Answer: MVC is a design pattern that separates an application into three interconnected components: Model (data and logic), View (presentation), and Controller (user interaction).

71.   **What is the Singleton design pattern?**

Answer: The Singleton pattern ensures that a class has only one instance and provides a global point of access to that instance.

72.   **What is the Observer design pattern?**

Answer: The Observer pattern defines a one-to-many dependency between objects, where one object (the subject) maintains a list of its dependents (observers) and notifies them of state changes.

73.   **What is object-oriented programming (OOP)?**

Answer: OOP is a programming paradigm that uses objects and classes to represent and model real-world entities and their interactions in software.

74. **What are the four principles of OOP?**

Answer: The four principles of OOP are encapsulation, inheritance, polymorphism, and abstraction.

75. **What is inheritance in OOP?**

Answer: Inheritance is a mechanism that allows a new class to inherit the properties and methods of an existing class.

76. **What is abstraction in OOP?**

Answer: Abstraction is the process of simplifying complex reality by modeling classes based on their essential characteristics.

77. **What is an abstract class in OOP?**

Answer: An abstract class is a class that cannot be instantiated and is used as a base for other classes. It may contain abstract methods that are implemented by its subclasses.

78. **What is an interface in OOP?**

Answer: An interface is a contract that defines a set of methods that a class must implement. It allows multiple inheritance of method signatures.

79. **What is dynamic programming?**

Answer: Dynamic programming is a technique for solving complex problems by breaking them down into simpler subproblems and storing their solutions to avoid redundant computation.

80.   **What is a sorting algorithm?**

Answer: A sorting algorithm is an algorithm that arranges elements in a specific order, such as ascending or descending.

81.   **What is the bubble sort algorithm?**

Answer: Bubble sort is a simple sorting algorithm that repeatedly steps through the list, compares adjacent elements, and swaps them if they are in the wrong order.

82.   **What is the selection sort algorithm?**

Answer: Selection sort is a simple sorting algorithm that repeatedly selects the minimum element from an unsorted portion of the list and moves it to the sorted portion.

83.   **What is the insertion sort algorithm?**

Answer: Insertion sort is a simple sorting algorithm that builds the final sorted list one item at a time, inserting each item into its correct position.

84.   **What is a quicksort algorithm?**

Answer: Quicksort is a divide-and-conquer sorting algorithm that partitions the input into smaller segments and recursively sorts them. It is known for its efficiency.

85.   **What is a binary search algorithm?**

Answer: Binary search is a search algorithm that finds the position of a target value within a sorted array by repeatedly dividing the search interval in half.

86.   **What is a linked list in data structures?**

Answer: A linked list is a data structure in which elements, called nodes, are connected by pointers. It can be used to implement dynamic data structures.

87.   **What is a hash table in data structures?**

Answer: A hash table is a data structure that stores data in key-value pairs and uses a hash function to compute an index into an array of buckets or slots.

88.   **What is a graph in data structures?**

Answer: A graph is a data structure that consists of nodes (vertices) and edges, which connect pairs of nodes. It is used to model relationships between entities.

89.   **What is a tree in data structures?**

Answer: A tree is a hierarchical data structure with a root node and child nodes, organized in a branched structure. It is used for various applications, such as hierarchical data and searching.

90.   **What is an algorithm in programming?**

Answer: An algorithm is a step-by-step set of instructions for solving a specific problem or performing a particular task.

91. What is a time complexity of an algorithm?

Answer: Time complexity measures the amount of time an algorithm takes to run as a function of the input size.

92. What is a space complexity of an algorithm?

Answer: Space complexity measures the amount of memory an algorithm uses as a function of the input size.

93. What is the Big O notation in algorithm analysis?

Answer: Big O notation is used to describe the upper bound of the time or space complexity of an algorithm. It provides a way to compare algorithms based on their efficiency.

94. What is a software development life cycle (SDLC)?

Answer: The SDLC is a process for planning, creating, testing, and deploying software applications. It typically includes phases such as requirements, design, development, testing, and maintenance.

95. What is a user story in agile development?

Answer: A user story is a brief, plain language description of a software feature from an end user's perspective. It is used to capture requirements in agile development.

96. What is continuous integration (CI) in software development?

Answer: CI is a practice in which code changes are automatically built, tested, and integrated into a shared repository on a regular basis to ensure code quality and reduce integration issues.

97. What is the purpose of software testing?

Answer: Software testing is the process of evaluating a software application to identify and correct defects or issues, ensuring that it meets quality and performance standards.

98. What is a "data structure" in programming?

Answer: A data structure is a way to organize and store data for efficient access and manipulation.

99. What is a "linked list" in data structures?

Answer: A linked list is a linear data structure in which elements (nodes) are linked together by references, allowing for dynamic memory allocation.

100. What is a "tree" in data structures?

Answer: A tree is a hierarchical data structure with nodes connected in a branching structure, commonly used for organizing data.

101. What is "artificial intelligence" (AI)?

Answer: Artificial intelligence refers to the development of computer systems that can perform tasks that typically require human intelligence, such as problem-solving, learning, and decision-making.

102. What is "machine learning" in AI?

Answer: Machine learning is a subset of AI that involves training computer algorithms to improve their performance by learning from data and making predictions.

103. What is "deep learning" in AI?

Answer: Deep learning is a subset of machine learning that uses artificial neural networks with many layers (deep neural networks) to solve complex problems.

104. What is "natural language processing" (NLP) in AI?

Answer: Natural language processing is a field of AI that focuses on enabling machines to understand, interpret, and generate human language.

105. What is "reinforcement learning" in AI?

Answer: Reinforcement learning is a type of machine learning in which an agent learns to make decisions by taking actions in an environment and receiving feedback in the form of rewards.

106. Explain the concept of "unsupervised learning" in machine learning.

Answer: Unsupervised learning is a type of machine learning in which algorithms learn patterns and structures in data without labeled examples.

107. **What is "data mining" in data analysis?**

Answer: Data mining is the process of discovering patterns and insights from large datasets using techniques like clustering and association rule mining.

108. **What is "business intelligence" (BI)?**

Answer: Business intelligence refers to the technologies and processes used to collect, analyze, and present business data to support decision-making.

109. **What is "big data"?**

Answer: Big data refers to extremely large and complex datasets that are difficult to manage and analyze with traditional data processing tools.

110. **What is "data warehousing" in data management?**

Answer: Data warehousing involves centralizing data from various sources into a single repository for reporting and analysis.

111. **What is "data visualization" in data analysis?**

Answer: Data visualization is the graphical representation of data to make it easier to understand and derive insights.

112. **What is "binary search" in data structures?**

Answer: Binary search is an efficient algorithm for finding a specific value in a sorted list by repeatedly dividing the search interval in half.

113. **What is "dynamic programming" in algorithm design?**

Answer: Dynamic programming is an optimization technique used to solve problems by breaking them down into smaller subproblems and reusing solutions.

114. **What is "hashing" in data structures?**

Answer: Hashing is a technique that maps data to a fixed-size array, enabling efficient retrieval and storage of values.

115. **What is "recursion" in programming?**

116. **Answer:** Recursion is a technique where a function calls itself to solve problems that can be broken down into smaller instances of the same problem.

117. **What is "stack overflow" in programming?**

Answer: Stack overflow occurs when the call stack, a data structure for function calls, exceeds its capacity due to excessive recursion.

118. **What is "stack" and "heap" memory in programming?**

Answer: Stack memory is used for function call management and has a limited fixed size, while heap memory is used for dynamic memory allocation and has a larger, variable size.

119. **What is "garbage collection" in programming languages like Java?**

Answer: Garbage collection is the automatic process of reclaiming memory occupied by objects that are no longer in use to prevent memory leaks.

120. **What is "merge sort" in sorting algorithms?**

Answer: Merge sort is a comparison-based sorting algorithm that divides the input list into smaller sublists, sorts them, and merges the sorted sublists.

121. **What is "quick sort" in sorting algorithms?**

Answer: Quick sort is a fast, in-place sorting algorithm that selects a pivot element and rearranges the list such that elements smaller than the pivot are on its left and larger elements are on its right.

122. **What is "graph" in data structures?**

Answer: A graph is a collection of nodes connected by edges, used to represent relationships and connections.

123. **What is "breadth-first search" (BFS) in graph algorithms?**

Answer: Breadth-first search is an algorithm for traversing or searching a graph by exploring all neighbor nodes at the present depth before moving to nodes at the next depth.

124. **What is "depth-first search" (DFS) in graph algorithms?**

Answer: Depth-first search is an algorithm for traversing or searching a graph by exploring as far as possible along a branch before backtracking.

125.   **What is a "queue" in data structures?**

Answer: A queue is a linear data structure that follows the First-In-First-Out (FIFO) principle.

126.   **What is "vector" or "ArrayList" in programming languages like C++ and Java?**

Answer: A vector or ArrayList is a dynamic array that can grow or shrink in size to accommodate elements.

127.   **What is " polymorphism " in object-oriented programming?**

Answer: Polymorphism allows objects of different classes to be treated as objects of a common base class, simplifying code that works with multiple objects.

128.   **What is "abstraction" in object-oriented programming?**

Answer: Abstraction is the process of simplifying complex reality by modeling classes and objects in a way that hides unnecessary details.

129.   **What is "inheritance" in object-oriented programming?**

Answer: Inheritance allows a new class (subclass or derived class) to inherit properties and behaviors from an existing class (superclass or base class).

130.   **What is a "constructor" in object-oriented programming?**

Answer: A constructor is a special method used to initialize an object's state when it is created.

131. **What is "method overloading" in object-oriented programming?**

Answer: Method overloading is the ability to define multiple methods with the same name in a class, differing in the number or type of their parameters.

132. **What is "method overriding" in object-oriented programming?**

Answer: Method overriding allows a subclass to provide a specific implementation of a method that is already defined in its superclass.

133. **What is "composition" in object-oriented programming?**

Answer: Composition is a design technique where one class contains an instance of another class as a member, creating a "has-a" relationship.

134. **What is "static" and "instance" in class members in object-oriented programming?**

Answer: Static members belong to the class itself, while instance members belong to each instance (object) of the class.

135. **What is an "interface" in object-oriented programming?**

Answer: An interface defines a contract of methods that a class implementing the interface must provide, ensuring consistency in behavior.

136. What is "final" in programming languages like Java and C++?

Answer: The "final" keyword is used to indicate that a variable, method, or class cannot be changed, overridden, or extended, respectively.

137. What is "null" in programming?

Answer: "Null" represents the absence of a value or a reference to an object.

138. What is "throw" and "try-catch" in exception handling?

Answer: "Throw" is used to raise an exception, while "try-catch" is used to handle exceptions and provide error recovery.

139. What is "file I/O" in programming?

Answer: File I/O, or file input/output, involves reading and writing data to and from files on a computer's storage.

140. What is "serialization" in programming?

Answer: Serialization is the process of converting an object's state into a byte stream to be stored, transmitted, or reconstructed later.

141. What is "multithreading" in programming?

Answer: Multithreading is the concurrent execution of multiple threads to improve program performance and responsiveness.

142. **What is a "mutex" or "semaphore" in multithreading?**

Answer: A mutex or semaphore is a synchronization mechanism used to control access to shared resources in a multithreaded program.

143. **What is "deadlock" in multithreading?**

Answer: Deadlock occurs when two or more threads are unable to proceed because each is waiting for the other to release a resource.

144. **What is "race condition" in multithreading?**

Answer: A race condition occurs when the behavior of a program depends on the relative timing of events in concurrent execution.

145. **What is "fork" and "join" in parallel programming?**

Answer: "Fork" creates parallel tasks, and "join" waits for those tasks to complete and synchronize.

146. **What is "concurrency" in programming?**

Answer: Concurrency is the execution of multiple tasks simultaneously or in overlapping time periods.

147. **What is "asynchronous programming" in software development?**

Answer: Asynchronous programming allows tasks to run independently, enabling non-blocking operations and improving performance in applications.

148. **What is "thread pool" in multithreading?**

Answer: A thread pool is a collection of threads that can be reused to execute tasks, reducing the overhead of thread creation and destruction.

149. **What is "lambda expression" in programming languages like Java and C#?**

Answer: A lambda expression is a concise way to define anonymous functions or methods, often used for inline code blocks.

150. **What is "reflection" in programming?**

Answer: Reflection allows programs to inspect and manipulate their own structure, classes, methods, and fields at runtime.

151. **What is "unit testing" in software development?**

Answer: Unit testing involves testing individual components or functions in isolation to ensure they work correctly.

152. **What is "integration testing" in software development?**

Answer: Integration testing involves testing interactions between components or modules to ensure they work together as expected.

153. **What is "code review" in software development?**

Answer: Code review is the practice of examining and evaluating source code to identify defects, improve code quality, and share knowledge.

154. **What is "debugging" in software development?**

Answer: Debugging is the process of identifying and resolving errors or defects in software to make it work as intended.

155. **What is "refactoring" in software development?**

Answer: Refactoring involves making improvements to existing code without changing its external behavior to enhance maintainability and readability.

156. **What is "design pattern" in software development?**

Answer: A design pattern is a reusable and common solution to a specific problem in software design.

157. **What is "waterfall" and "agile" project management?**

Answer: Waterfall is a linear project management approach, while agile is an iterative and flexible approach that emphasizes collaboration and adaptability.

158. **What is "scrum" in agile project management?**

Answer: Scrum is an agile framework for managing and completing complex projects, emphasizing iterative development and frequent inspection.

159. **What is "Kanban" in agile project management?**

Answer: Kanban is an agile methodology that focuses on visualizing work, limiting work in progress, and optimizing the flow of work.

160. **What is "user story" in agile project management?**

Answer: A user story is a brief description of a software feature from an end user's perspective, used to express requirements in an agile project.

161. **What is "pair programming" in agile development?**

Answer: Pair programming involves two developers working together at a single computer, often with one writing code and the other reviewing.

162. **What is "continuous delivery" in software development?**

Answer: Continuous delivery is the practice of automatically deploying software changes to production when they pass automated tests and quality checks.

163. **What is "microservices architecture" in software development?**

Answer: Microservices architecture is an approach to building software systems as a collection of small, independently deployable services that work together.

164. **What is "serverless computing" in cloud computing?**

Answer: Serverless computing allows developers to run code in response to events without managing server infrastructure, focusing on code execution.

165.   **What is "NoSQL" in database management?**

Answer: NoSQL databases are non-relational databases designed to handle large amounts of unstructured or semi-structured data.

166.   **What is "CAP theorem" in distributed systems?**

Answer: The CAP theorem states that in a distributed system, it is impossible to guarantee all three of Consistency, Availability, and Partition tolerance simultaneously.

167.   **What is "container orchestration" in cloud computing?**

Answer: Container orchestration is the automated management and scaling of containers in a cluster to ensure applications run reliably and efficiently.

168.   **What is "micro-frontends" in web development?**

Answer: Micro-frontends is an architectural approach where the front-end of a web application is divided into smaller, independent components.

169.   **What is "server-side rendering" (SSR) in web development?**

Answer: Server-side rendering is a technique in which web pages are rendered on the server before being sent to the client, improving initial page load performance.

170. **What is "client-side rendering" (CSR) in web development?**

Answer: Client-side rendering is a technique where web pages are rendered in the user's browser, allowing for dynamic and interactive content.

171. **What is "single-page application" (SPA) in web development?**

Answer: A single-page application is a web application that loads a single HTML page and dynamically updates the content, providing a seamless user experience.

172. **What is "content delivery network" (CDN) in web development?**

Answer: A CDN is a network of servers distributed geographically to deliver web content, such as images and videos, more efficiently to users.

173. **What is "progressive web app" (PWA) in web development?**

Answer: A PWA is a web application that provides a native app-like experience and can work offline or with a poor internet connection.

174. **What is "RESTful API" in web development?**

Answer: A RESTful API is an architectural style for designing networked applications that use HTTP requests to perform CRUD (Create, Read, Update, Delete) operations.

175. What is "GraphQL" in web development?

Answer: GraphQL is a query language and runtime for APIs that allows clients to request only the data they need, reducing over-fetching and under-fetching.

176. What is "cookie" and "session" in web development?

Answer: Cookies are small pieces of data stored in a user's browser, while sessions are server-side data used to maintain state between web requests.

177. What is "cross-site scripting" (XSS) in web security?

Answer: Cross-site scripting is a security vulnerability in which attackers inject malicious scripts into web pages viewed by other users, often stealing sensitive data.

178. What is "SQL injection" in web security?

Answer: SQL injection is a security vulnerability that occurs when an attacker inserts malicious SQL code into input fields to gain unauthorized access to a database.

179. What is "ransomware" in cybersecurity?

Answer: Ransomware is a type of malware that encrypts a victim's data and demands a ransom for the decryption key.

180. **What is "phishing" in cybersecurity?**

Answer: Phishing is a cyberattack in which attackers use fraudulent emails or messages to trick individuals into revealing sensitive information.

181. **What is "two-factor authentication" (2FA) in cybersecurity?**

Answer: Two-factor authentication requires users to provide two different authentication factors to access a system or account, enhancing security.

182. **What is "malware" in cybersecurity?**

Answer: Malware is malicious software designed to harm or exploit computer systems and users, including viruses, worms, and spyware.

183. **What is "white hat hacking" in cybersecurity?**

Answer: White hat hacking, or ethical hacking, involves security experts testing systems for vulnerabilities with the owner's permission to improve security.

184. **What is "black hat hacking" in cybersecurity?**

Answer: Black hat hacking involves individuals or groups exploiting vulnerabilities for malicious purposes without authorization.

185. **What is "social engineering" in cybersecurity?**

Answer: Social engineering is a technique in which attackers manipulate individuals to divulge sensitive information or perform actions.

186. **What is "zero-day vulnerability" in cybersecurity?**

Answer: A zero-day vulnerability is a security flaw that is exploited by attackers before the responsible party can fix it.

187. **What is "penetration testing" in cybersecurity?**

Answer: Penetration testing involves ethical hackers simulating real-world cyberattacks to identify vulnerabilities in a system or network.

188. **What is "blockchain" technology, and how does it work?**

Answer: Blockchain is a distributed ledger technology that securely records transactions in a tamper-resistant manner using linked data blocks.

189. **What is "decentralized finance" (DeFi) in blockchain and cryptocurrency?**

Answer: DeFi refers to a financial system built on blockchain technology that offers traditional financial services without centralized intermediaries.

190. **What is "tokenization" in blockchain technology?**

Answer: Tokenization involves converting real or digital assets into digital tokens that can be bought, sold, or traded on blockchain platforms.

191. **What is "smart property" in blockchain technology?**

Answer: Smart property refers to physical or digital assets that are digitally managed and controlled using blockchain technology and smart contracts.

192. **What is a "smart city" in the context of technology and urban planning?**

Answer: A smart city uses technology and data to improve the efficiency, sustainability, and quality of life for its residents.

193. **What is "quantum computing"?**

Answer: Quantum computing is an emerging field of computing that uses the principles of quantum mechanics to perform calculations much faster than classical computers.

194. **What is "quantum supremacy" in quantum computing?**

Answer: Quantum supremacy is the point at which a quantum computer can perform tasks that are practically impossible for classical computers to complete within a reasonable timeframe.

195. **What is "quantum entanglement" in quantum physics?**

Answer: Quantum entanglement is a phenomenon where particles become correlated in a way that the state of one particle depends on the state of another, even when separated by large distances.

196. **What is "quantum superposition" in quantum physics?**

Answer: Quantum superposition is the ability of quantum particles to exist in multiple states simultaneously until measured, a fundamental principle of quantum mechanics.

197.   **What is "quantum teleportation" in quantum physics?**

Answer: Quantum teleportation is a process by which the quantum state of one particle can be transmitted to another, even over long distances.

198.   **What is "quantum cryptography" in quantum technology?**

Answer: Quantum cryptography uses quantum properties to secure communication, making it theoretically impossible for eavesdroppers to intercept messages without detection.

199.   **What is "quantum key distribution" (QKD) in quantum cryptography?**

Answer: Quantum key distribution uses quantum properties to securely exchange cryptographic keys for encrypted communication.

200.   **What is "quantum error correction" in quantum computing?**

Answer: Quantum error correction is a set of techniques and algorithms that help protect quantum information from errors due to environmental factors.

201.   **What is "quantum algorithm" in quantum computing?**

Answer: A quantum algorithm is a set of instructions for performing computations on a quantum computer, often designed to outperform classical algorithms.

202. **What is "quantum machine learning" in quantum computing?**

Answer: Quantum machine learning is the application of quantum computing to enhance machine learning algorithms, potentially solving complex problems more efficiently.

203. **What is "quantum annealing" in quantum computing?**

Answer: Quantum annealing is a quantum computing technique for finding the global minimum of a function, with applications in optimization problems.

204. **What is "quantum supremacy" in quantum computing?**

Answer: Quantum supremacy is the point at which a quantum computer can perform tasks that are practically impossible for classical computers to complete within a reasonable timeframe.

205. **What is the purpose of a constructor in Java?**

Answer: A constructor in Java is used to initialize an object's state when it is created.

206. **What does the term "IDE" stand for in software development?**

Answer: IDE stands for "Integrated Development Environment," which is a software suite that provides tools for coding, debugging, and building applications.

207. **What is version control in software development?**

Answer: Version control is a system that tracks and manages changes to source code, allowing multiple developers to collaborate on a project.

208. **What is a "stack" and a "queue" in data structures?**

Answer: A stack is a data structure that follows the Last-In-First-Out (LIFO) principle, while a queue follows the First-In-First-Out (FIFO) principle.

209. **What is the difference between "compilation" and "interpretation" in programming languages?**

Answer: Compilation translates the entire source code into machine code before execution, while interpretation translates and executes code line by line.

210. **What is "inheritance" in object-oriented programming?**

Answer: Inheritance allows a new class (subclass or derived class) to inherit properties and behaviors from an existing class (superclass or base class).

211. **Explain the difference between "static" and "dynamic" typing in programming languages.**

Answer: Static typing requires variable types to be declared at compile time, while dynamic typing determines types at runtime.

212. **What is "object serialization" in programming?**

Answer: Object serialization is the process of converting an object's state into a byte stream to be stored, transmitted, or reconstructed later.

213. **What is a "binary search" algorithm?**

Answer: Binary search is an efficient algorithm for finding a specific value in a sorted list by repeatedly dividing the search interval in half.

214. **What is the "Big O" notation in algorithm analysis?**

Answer: Big O notation is used to describe the upper bound of an algorithm's time or space complexity in terms of input size.

215. **What is "agile" software development?**

Answer: Agile is an iterative and flexible approach to software development that emphasizes collaboration, customer feedback, and adaptability.

216. **Explain the concept of "database normalization."**

Answer: Database normalization is the process of organizing data in a database to reduce redundancy and improve data integrity.

217. **What is "scrum" in agile project management?**

Answer: Scrum is an agile framework for managing and completing complex projects, emphasizing iterative development, frequent inspection, and adaptation.

218. **What is "responsive web design"?**

Answer: Responsive web design is an approach that ensures web pages adapt to different screen sizes and devices, providing an optimal user experience.

219. **What is a "kernel" in operating systems?**

Answer: The kernel is the core component of an operating system responsible for managing hardware resources and providing essential services.

220. **Explain the concept of "virtual memory" in operating systems.**

Answer: Virtual memory is a memory management technique that allows the use of more memory than is physically available by swapping data between RAM and disk.

221. **What is a "file system" in operating systems?**

Answer: A file system is a method for storing and organizing files on a storage medium, such as a hard drive.

222. **What is "network latency"?**

Answer: Network latency is the delay in data transmission between two points in a network and can affect the responsiveness of networked applications.

223. **Explain the concept of "packet switching" in networking.**

Answer: Packet switching is a method of data transmission where data is divided into packets for efficient and shared use of network resources.

224. **What is "DNS" in networking?**

Answer: DNS, or Domain Name System, is a system that translates human-readable domain names into IP addresses used by computers to locate resources on the internet.

225. **What is a "firewall" in network security?**

Answer: A firewall is a security device or software that controls network traffic and enforces access policies to protect against unauthorized access and threats.

226. **What is "symmetric encryption" in cryptography?**

Answer: Symmetric encryption uses the same key for both encryption and decryption, making it efficient but requiring secure key distribution.

227. **What is "asymmetric encryption" in cryptography?**

Answer: Asymmetric encryption uses a pair of keys (public and private) for encryption and decryption, providing secure communication and digital signatures.

228. **What is "blockchain" technology, and how does it work?**

Answer: Blockchain is a distributed ledger technology that records transactions in a secure and tamper-resistant manner by linking data in blocks and using cryptographic techniques.

229. **Explain the concept of "smart contracts" in blockchain technology.**

Answer: Smart contracts are self-executing contracts that automatically enforce terms and conditions using blockchain technology.

230. **What is "cryptocurrency"?**

Answer: Cryptocurrency is a digital or virtual form of currency that uses cryptography for security and operates independently of a central authority, like a central bank.

231. **What is "DevOps" in software development?**

Answer: DevOps is a set of practices that aims to improve collaboration between software development (Dev) and IT operations (Ops) to enhance the software delivery process.

232. **What is "containerization" in software development?**

Answer: Containerization is a technology that packages an application and its dependencies into a container, making it portable and consistent across different environments.

233. **What is "microservices architecture" in software development?**

Answer: Microservices architecture is an approach to building software systems as a collection of small, independently deployable services that work together.

234. **What is "NoSQL" in database management?**

Answer: NoSQL databases are non-relational databases designed to handle large amounts of unstructured or semi-structured data.

235. **What is "CAP theorem" in distributed systems?**

Answer: The CAP theorem states that in a distributed system, it is impossible to guarantee all three of Consistency, Availability, and Partition tolerance simultaneously.

236. **What is "container orchestration" in cloud computing?**

Answer: Container orchestration is the automated management and scaling of containers in a cluster to ensure applications run reliably and efficiently.

237. **Explain the concept of "server-side rendering" (SSR) in web development.**

Answer: Server-side rendering is a technique in which web pages are rendered on the server before being sent to the client, improving initial page load performance.

238. **What is "progressive web app" (PWA) in web development?**

Answer: A PWA is a web application that provides a native app-like experience and can work offline or with a poor internet connection.

239. **What is "server-side scripting" in web development?**

Answer: Server-side scripting is the execution of code on the web server to generate dynamic web content before it is sent to the client's browser.

240. **What is "client-side scripting" in web development?**

Answer: Client-side scripting is the execution of code in the user's web browser to create dynamic web content and interactivity.

241. **What is "user experience" (UX) design in web development?**

Answer: UX design focuses on creating a positive and enjoyable experience for users when interacting with websites and applications.

242. **What is "user interface" (UI) design in web development?**

Answer: UI design involves creating the visual and interactive elements of a website or application to ensure a user-friendly interface.

243. **What is "A/B testing" in web development and marketing?**

Answer: A/B testing is a method of comparing two versions (A and B) of a web page or element to determine which performs better with users.

244. **What is "responsive web design" in web development?**

Answer: Responsive web design is an approach that ensures web pages adapt to different screen sizes and devices, providing an optimal user experience.

245. **What is "ransomware" in cybersecurity?**

Answer: Ransomware is a type of malware that encrypts a victim's data and demands a ransom for the decryption key.

246. **What is "two-factor authentication" (2FA) in cybersecurity?**

Answer: Two-factor authentication requires users to provide two different authentication factors to access a system or account, enhancing security.

247. **What is "white hat hacking" in cybersecurity?**

Answer: White hat hacking, or ethical hacking, involves security experts testing systems for vulnerabilities with the owner's permission to improve security.

248. **What is "black hat hacking" in cybersecurity?**

Answer: Black hat hacking involves individuals or groups exploiting vulnerabilities for malicious purposes without authorization.

249. **What is "social engineering" in cybersecurity?**

Answer: Social engineering is a technique in which attackers manipulate individuals to divulge sensitive information or perform actions.

250. **What is "zero-day vulnerability" in cybersecurity?**

Answer: A zero-day vulnerability is a security flaw that is exploited by attackers before the responsible party can fix it.

251. **What is "penetration testing" in cybersecurity?**

Answer: Penetration testing involves ethical hackers simulating real-world cyberattacks to identify vulnerabilities in a system or network.

252. **What is "blockchain" technology, and how does it work?**

Answer: Blockchain is a distributed ledger technology that securely records transactions in a tamper-resistant manner using linked data blocks.

253. **What is "decentralized finance" (DeFi) in blockchain and cryptocurrency?**

Answer: DeFi refers to a financial system built on blockchain technology that offers traditional financial services without centralized intermediaries.

254. **What is "tokenization" in blockchain technology?**

Answer: Tokenization involves converting real or digital assets into digital tokens that can be bought, sold, or traded on blockchain platforms.

255. **What is "smart property" in blockchain technology?**

Answer: Smart property refers to physical or digital assets that are digitally managed and controlled using blockchain technology and smart contracts.

256. **What is a "smart city" in the context of technology and urban planning?**

Answer: A smart city uses technology and data to improve the efficiency, sustainability, and quality of life for its residents.

257. **What is "object detection" in computer vision?**

Answer: Object detection is the process of locating and classifying objects within images or video.

258. **What is "natural language generation" (NLG) in AI?**

Answer: Natural language generation involves AI systems generating human-readable text or content.

259. **What is "recommender systems" in AI?**

Answer: Recommender systems use algorithms to suggest products, content, or services based on a user's preferences or behavior.

260. **What is "data preprocessing" in machine learning?**

Answer: Data preprocessing involves cleaning, transforming, and organizing data to prepare it for machine learning algorithms.

261. **What is "overfitting" in machine learning?**

Answer: Overfitting occurs when a machine learning model performs well on training data but poorly on new, unseen data, indicating it has learned noise in the data.

262. **What is "cross-validation" in machine learning?**

Answer: Cross-validation is a technique for assessing the performance of a machine learning model by partitioning data into subsets for training and testing.

263. **What is "ensemble learning" in machine learning?**

Answer: Ensemble learning combines the predictions of multiple machine learning models to improve overall performance.

264. **What is "data augmentation" in deep learning and computer vision?**

Answer: Data augmentation involves creating variations of training data to improve the performance and generalization of deep learning models.

265. **What is "bias" and "variance" in machine learning?**

Answer: Bias refers to the error due to overly simplistic assumptions in the learning algorithm, while variance is the error due to excessive complexity.

266. **What is "precision" and "recall" in classification tasks?**

Answer: Precision is the ratio of true positive predictions to the total positive predictions, and recall is the ratio of true positives to the total actual positives.

267. **What is "dimensionality reduction" in machine learning?**

Answer: Dimensionality reduction techniques reduce the number of input features or dimensions in a dataset while retaining relevant information.

268. **What is "transfer learning" in deep learning?**

Answer: Transfer learning involves using a pre-trained neural network as the starting point for a new task, often improving model performance.

269. **What is "GPT" in the context of natural language processing and AI?**

Answer: GPT, or "Generative Pre-trained Transformer," is a type of AI model used for tasks like text generation and language understanding.

270. **What is "quantum entanglement" in quantum physics?**

Answer: Quantum entanglement is a phenomenon where particles become correlated in a way that the state of one particle depends on the state of another, even when separated by large distances.

271. **What is "quantum superposition" in quantum physics?**

Answer: Quantum superposition is the ability of quantum particles to exist in multiple states simultaneously until measured, a fundamental principle of quantum mechanics.

272. **What is "quantum teleportation" in quantum physics?**

Answer: Quantum teleportation is a process by which the quantum state of one particle can be transmitted to another, even over long distances.

273. **What is "quantum cryptography" in quantum technology?**

Answer: Quantum cryptography uses quantum properties to secure communication, making it theoretically impossible for eavesdroppers to intercept messages without detection.

274. **What is "quantum key distribution" (QKD) in quantum cryptography?**

Answer: Quantum key distribution uses quantum properties to securely exchange cryptographic keys for encrypted communication.

275. **What is "quantum error correction" in quantum computing?**

Answer: Quantum error correction is a set of techniques and algorithms that help protect quantum information from errors due to environmental factors.

276. **What is "quantum algorithm" in quantum computing?**

Answer: A quantum algorithm is a set of instructions for performing computations on a quantum computer, often designed to outperform classical algorithms.

277. **What is "quantum machine learning" in quantum computing?**

Answer: Quantum machine learning is the application of quantum computing to enhance machine learning algorithms, potentially solving complex problems more efficiently.

278. **What is "quantum annealing" in quantum computing?**

Answer: Quantum annealing is a quantum computing technique for finding the global minimum of a function, with applications in optimization problems.

279. **What is "quantum supremacy" in quantum computing?**

Answer: Quantum supremacy is the point at which a quantum computer can perform tasks that are practically impossible for classical computers to complete within a reasonable timeframe.

280. **What is "virtual reality" (VR) technology?**

Answer: Virtual reality technology immerses users in a computer-generated environment, often using headsets and controllers.

281. **What is "mixed reality" (MR) technology?**

Answer: Mixed reality combines elements of both virtual reality and augmented reality to create immersive and interactive experiences.

282. **What is "holography" in visual technology?**

Answer: Holography is a technique that captures and displays 3D images, creating an illusion of depth without the need for special glasses.

283. **What is "3D printing" technology?**

Answer: 3D printing is a process of creating physical objects from digital models by adding material layer by layer.

284. **What is "artificial intelligence" (AI) in healthcare?**

Answer: AI in healthcare involves the use of machine learning and data analysis to improve patient care, diagnostics, and administrative tasks.

285. **What is "telemedicine" in healthcare?**

Answer: Telemedicine allows patients to receive medical care remotely through digital communication tools, reducing the need for in-person visits.

286. **What is "wearable technology" in healthcare?**

Answer: Wearable technology includes devices like fitness trackers and smartwatches that monitor health metrics and activity levels.

287. **What is "personalized medicine" in healthcare?**

Answer: Personalized medicine tailors medical treatments to an individual's genetics, lifestyle, and specific health characteristics.

288.   **What is "telehealth" in healthcare?**

Answer: Telehealth is a broad term that encompasses the use of telecommunications and information technology to provide healthcare services remotely.

289.   **What is "genetic engineering" in biotechnology?**

Answer: Genetic engineering involves modifying an organism's genetic material to achieve desired traits or outcomes.

290.   **What is "gene editing" using CRISPR-Cas9 technology?**

Answer: Gene editing with CRISPR-Cas9 is a precise method for altering DNA sequences, potentially treating genetic diseases and more.

291.   **What is "biometrics" in security and identification?**

Answer: Biometrics involves using unique physical or behavioral traits, like fingerprints or facial recognition, for authentication and identification.

292.   **What is "blockchain" in supply chain management?**

Answer: Blockchain technology can improve supply chain transparency, traceability, and security by recording transactions in a tamper-resistant ledger.

293.   **What is "virtual private network" (VPN) technology?**

Answer: A VPN creates a secure, encrypted connection over a public network, protecting data and providing online anonymity.

294.   **What is "5G" technology in telecommunications?**

Answer: 5G is the fifth generation of wireless technology, offering faster data speeds, lower latency, and support for emerging technologies.

295.   **What is "Internet of Things" (IoT) technology?**

Answer: IoT technology connects devices and sensors to the internet, allowing them to collect and exchange data for various applications.

296.   **What is "big data" in technology and data analysis?**

Answer: Big data refers to the large volume, velocity, and variety of data that can be analyzed to reveal patterns, trends, and insights.

297.   **What is "data analytics" in business and technology?**

Answer: Data analytics involves examining data to discover meaningful insights, make informed decisions, and drive business improvements.

298.   **What is "cloud computing" technology?**

Answer: Cloud computing provides on-demand access to computing resources over the internet, enabling scalable and flexible services.

299.   **What is "IaaS," "PaaS," and "SaaS" in cloud service models?**

Answer: IaaS (Infrastructure as a Service) provides virtualized computing resources, PaaS (Platform as a Service) offers development and deployment platforms, and SaaS (Software as a Service) delivers software applications via the cloud.

300. **What is "microservices architecture" in software development?**

Answer: Microservices architecture is an approach to building software systems as a collection of small, independently deployable services that work together.

301. **What is "server-side rendering" (SSR) in web development?**

Answer: Server-side rendering is a technique in which web pages are rendered on the server before being sent to the client, improving initial page load performance.

302. **What is a "single-page application" (SPA) in web development?**

Answer: A single-page application is a web application that loads a single HTML page and dynamically updates the content, providing a seamless user experience.

303. **What is "content delivery network" (CDN) in web development?**

Answer: A CDN is a network of servers distributed geographically to deliver web content, such as images and videos, more efficiently to users.

304. **What is "progressive web app" (PWA) in web development?**

Answer: A PWA is a web application that provides a native app-like experience and can work offline or with a poor internet connection.

305. **What is "RESTful API" in web development?**

Answer: A RESTful API is an architectural style for designing networked applications that use HTTP requests to perform CRUD (Create, Read, Update, Delete) operations.

306. **What is "GraphQL" in web development?**

Answer: GraphQL is a query language and runtime for APIs that allows clients to request only the data they need, reducing over-fetching and under-fetching.

307. **What is "cookie" and "session" in web development?**

Answer: Cookies are small pieces of data stored in a user's browser, while sessions are server-side data used to maintain state between web requests.

308. **What is "ransomware" in cybersecurity?**

Answer: Ransomware is a type of malware that encrypts a victim's data and demands a ransom for the decryption key.

309. **What is "phishing" in cybersecurity?**

Answer: Phishing is a cyberattack in which attackers use fraudulent emails or messages to trick individuals into revealing sensitive information.

310.   **What is "malware" in cybersecurity?**

Answer: Malware is malicious software designed to harm or exploit computer systems and users, including viruses, worms, and spyware.

311.   **What is "white hat hacking" in cybersecurity?**

Answer: White hat hacking, or ethical hacking, involves security experts testing systems for vulnerabilities with the owner's permission to improve security.

312.   **What is "black hat hacking" in cybersecurity?**

Answer: Black hat hacking involves individuals or groups exploiting vulnerabilities for malicious purposes without authorization.

313.   **What is "social engineering" in cybersecurity?**

Answer: Social engineering is a technique in which attackers manipulate individuals to divulge sensitive information or perform actions.

314.   **What is "zero-day vulnerability" in cybersecurity?**

Answer: A zero-day vulnerability is a security flaw that is exploited by attackers before the responsible party can fix it.

315.   **What is "penetration testing" in cybersecurity?**

Answer: Penetration testing involves ethical hackers simulating real-world cyberattacks to identify vulnerabilities in a system or network.

316. **What is "blockchain" technology, and how does it work?**

Answer: Blockchain is a distributed ledger technology that securely records transactions in a tamper-resistant manner using linked data blocks.

317. **What is "decentralized finance" (DeFi) in blockchain and cryptocurrency?**

Answer: DeFi refers to a financial system built on blockchain technology that offers traditional financial services without centralized intermediaries.

318. **What is "tokenization" in blockchain technology?**

Answer: Tokenization involves converting real or digital assets into digital tokens that can be bought, sold, or traded on blockchain platforms.

319. **What is "smart property" in blockchain technology?**

Answer: Smart property refers to physical or digital assets that are digitally managed and controlled using blockchain technology and smart contracts.

320. **What is a "smart city" in the context of technology and urban planning?**

Answer: A smart city uses technology and data to improve the efficiency, sustainability, and quality of life for its residents.

321. **What is "quantum computing"?**

Answer: Quantum computing is an emerging field of computing that uses the principles of quantum mechanics to perform calculations much faster than classical computers.

322. **What is "quantum supremacy" in quantum computing?**

Answer: Quantum supremacy is the point at which a quantum computer can perform tasks that are practically impossible for classical computers to complete within a reasonable timeframe.

323. **What is "quantum entanglement" in quantum physics?**

Answer: Quantum entanglement is a phenomenon where particles become correlated in a way that the state of one particle depends on the state of another, even when separated by large distances.

324. **What is "quantum superposition" in quantum physics?**

Answer: Quantum superposition is the ability of quantum particles to exist in multiple states simultaneously until measured, a fundamental principle of quantum mechanics.

325. **What is "quantum teleportation" in quantum physics?**

Answer: Quantum teleportation is a process by which the quantum state of one particle can be transmitted to another, even over long distances.

326. **What is "quantum cryptography" in quantum technology?**

Answer: Quantum cryptography uses quantum properties to secure communication, making it theoretically impossible for eavesdroppers to intercept messages without detection.

327. **What is "quantum key distribution" (QKD) in quantum cryptography?**

Answer: Quantum key distribution uses quantum properties to securely exchange cryptographic keys for encrypted communication.

328. **What is "quantum error correction" in quantum computing?**

Answer: Quantum error correction is a set of techniques and algorithms that help protect quantum information from errors due to environmental factors.

329. **What is "quantum annealing" in quantum computing?**

Answer: Quantum annealing is a quantum computing technique for finding the global minimum of a function, with applications in optimization problems.

330. **What is "quantum supremacy" in quantum computing?**

Answer: Quantum supremacy is the point at which a quantum computer can perform tasks that are practically impossible for classical computers to complete within a reasonable timeframe.

331. **What is "augmented reality" (AR) technology?**

Answer: Augmented reality technology overlays digital content onto the real world, typically viewed through smartphones or AR glasses.

332. **What is "holography" in visual technology?**

Answer: Holography is a technique that captures and displays 3D images, creating an illusion of depth without the need for special glasses.

333. **What is "telemedicine" in healthcare?**

Answer: Telemedicine allows patients to receive medical care remotely through digital communication tools, reducing the need for in-person visits.

334. **What is "wearable technology" in healthcare?**

Answer: Wearable technology includes devices like fitness trackers and smartwatches that monitor health metrics and activity levels.

335. **What is "personalized medicine" in healthcare?**

Answer: Personalized medicine tailors medical treatments to an individual's genetics, lifestyle, and specific health characteristics.

336. **What is "telehealth" in healthcare?**

Answer: Telehealth is a broad term that encompasses the use of telecommunications and information technology to provide healthcare services remotely.

337. **What is "genetic engineering" in biotechnology?**

Answer: Genetic engineering involves modifying an organism's genetic material to achieve desired traits or outcomes.

338. **What is "gene editing" using CRISPR-Cas9 technology?**

Answer: Gene editing with CRISPR-Cas9 is a precise method for altering DNA sequences, potentially treating genetic diseases and more.

339. **What is "biometrics" in security and identification?**

Answer: Biometrics involves using unique physical or behavioral traits, like fingerprints or facial recognition, for authentication and identification.

340. **What is "blockchain" in supply chain management?**

Answer: Blockchain technology can improve supply chain transparency, traceability, and security by recording transactions in a tamper-resistant ledger.

341. **What is "virtual private network" (VPN) technology?**

Answer: A VPN creates a secure, encrypted connection over a public network, protecting data and providing online anonymity.

342. **What is "5G" technology in telecommunications?**

Answer: 5G is the fifth generation of wireless technology, offering faster data speeds, lower latency, and support for emerging technologies.

343. **What is "Internet of Things" (IoT) technology?**

Answer: IoT technology connects devices and sensors to the internet, allowing them to collect and exchange data for various applications.

344. What is "data analytics" in business and technology?

Answer: Data analytics involves examining data to discover meaningful insights, make informed decisions, and drive business improvements.

345. What is "data warehouse" in technology and data management?

Answer: A data warehouse is a centralized repository for storing, managing, and analyzing large volumes of data from various sources.

346. What is "IaaS," "PaaS," and "SaaS" in cloud service models?

Answer: IaaS (Infrastructure as a Service) provides virtualized computing resources, PaaS (Platform as a Service) offers development and deployment platforms, and SaaS (Software as a Service) delivers software applications via the cloud.

347. What is "microservices architecture" in software development?

Answer: Microservices architecture is an approach to building software systems as a collection of small, independently deployable services that work together.

348. What is a "single-page application" (SPA) in web development?

Answer: A single-page application is a web application that loads a single HTML page and dynamically updates the content, providing a seamless user experience.

349. **What is "content delivery network" (CDN) in web development?**

Answer: A CDN is a network of servers distributed geographically to deliver web content, such as images and videos, more efficiently to users.

350. **What is the purpose of a software requirement specification (SRS)?**

Answer: An SRS is a document that specifies the functional and non-functional requirements of a software system. It serves as a foundation for software design and development by providing a clear and comprehensive description of what the software should do.

351. **What are the advantages of using version control in a team environment?**

Answer: Version control (or source code control) systems, such as Git, provide benefits like collaboration, change tracking, and backup. In a team environment, advantages include:

Concurrent development and collaboration.

History and change tracking for code.

The ability to revert to previous versions.

Easy branching and merging for feature development.

Backup and disaster recovery.

352. What is an algorithm's time complexity?

Answer: Time complexity is a measure of the amount of time an algorithm takes to run based on the size of its input. It's often expressed using Big O notation to describe the upper bound of how the runtime grows with input size.

353. What is an algorithm's space complexity?

Answer: Space complexity is a measure of the amount of memory or space an algorithm uses as a function of the input size. It's used to analyze how much memory the algorithm requires.

354. What is a binary search tree (BST)?

Answer: A binary search tree is a data structure consisting of nodes where each node has at most two child nodes. The key (value) of a node is greater than or equal to the keys of all nodes in its left subtree and less than or equal to the keys of all nodes in its right subtree. This property allows efficient searching and sorting.

355. Explain the concept of an AVL tree.

Answer: An AVL tree (Adelson-Velsky and Landis tree) is a self-balancing binary search tree. It maintains a balance factor for each node (the difference in heights between the left and right subtrees) and ensures that this balance factor is within a limited range, typically -1, 0, or 1. This balance factor ensures that the tree remains balanced, preventing degeneration into a linked list, and keeping search operations efficient.

356. What is a hash function in the context of data structures?

Answer: A hash function is a function that takes an input (or "key") and produces a fixed-size string of characters, typically a hexadecimal number. It is used to map data to a location in a hash table or an array, allowing for efficient retrieval and storage of data.

357. What are getter and setter methods in Java?

Answer: Getter and setter methods (also known as accessor and mutator methods) are used in Java to access and modify the private fields (instance variables) of a class. Getter methods retrieve the values, while setter methods set new values for these fields, encapsulating the data and providing control over access and modification.

358. Explain the concept of dynamic programming.

Answer: Dynamic programming is a problem-solving technique used in computer science and mathematics. It involves solving complex problems by breaking them down into simpler, overlapping subproblems and storing the results of these subproblems to avoid redundant computations. Dynamic programming is particularly useful for optimization problems.

359. What is the purpose of the "break" statement in a loop?

Answer: The "break" statement is used in loops to exit the loop prematurely. When the "break" statement is encountered, the loop immediately terminates, and control flows to the statement after the loop.

360. How is memory management handled in modern programming languages?

Answer: Memory management in modern programming languages is typically automated. Languages like Java, C#, and Python use automatic memory management with mechanisms like garbage collection, which automatically deallocates memory when objects are no longer in use. This helps prevent memory leaks and makes memory management easier for developers.

361. What is a callback function in JavaScript?

Answer: A callback function is a function that is passed as an argument to another function and is executed after the completion of the outer function. Callbacks are often used to handle asynchronous operations, such as reading a file or making an HTTP request, and are central to event-driven and non-blocking programming in JavaScript.

362. What are the differences between the "==" and "===" operators in JavaScript?

Answer: In JavaScript, "==" is a loose equality operator that compares values for equality, while "===" is a strict equality operator that compares both values and types for equality. For example, "5 == '5'" is true (loose equality), but "5 === '5'" is false (strict equality) because they have different types.

363. What is the "prototype" in JavaScript?

Answer: In JavaScript, the "prototype" is an object that is associated with a constructor function or a class. It is used to define shared properties and methods for objects created from that constructor function or class. This enables inheritance and the sharing of functionality among objects.

364. What is an asynchronous function in JavaScript?

Answer: An asynchronous function in JavaScript is a function that does not block the program's execution while waiting for a time-consuming operation to complete, such as reading a file or making a network request. Instead, it allows other code to run concurrently and specifies a callback function to execute when the operation is finished.

365. How does garbage collection work in programming languages like Java?

Answer: Garbage collection is the process of automatically reclaiming memory that is no longer in use by the program. In languages like Java, this is done by the garbage collector, which periodically identifies and deallocates memory that is no longer reachable or referenced by the program.

366. What is a linked list in data structures?

369. **Describe the purpose of a software design pattern.**

Answer: Software design patterns are general reusable solutions to common problems encountered in software design. They provide templates for solving specific design and architectural challenges, improving code maintainability and scalability. Patterns like Singleton, Factory, and Observer are examples of well-known design patterns.

370. **What is the Singleton design pattern?**

Answer: The Singleton pattern ensures that a class has only one instance and provides a global point of access to that instance. It's often used for situations where a single point of control or coordination is needed, such as managing configurations or resources.

371. **Explain the Observer design pattern.**

Answer: The Observer pattern defines a one-to-many dependency between objects, where one object (the subject) maintains a list of its dependents (observers) and notifies them of state changes. This allows multiple objects to be notified and updated when the subject's state changes, promoting loose coupling.

372. **What is the purpose of the "finally" block in a try-catch-finally construct?**

Answer: In exception handling, the "finally" block is used to specify a block of code that is always executed, whether or not an exception is thrown in the "try" block. It is commonly used for resource cleanup, ensuring that resources are released, even in the presence of exceptions.

Answer: A linked list is a linear data structure that consists of a sequence of elements, where each element (node) points to the next element. It is used for dynamic data storage and allows for efficient insertions and deletions. Linked lists come in various forms, including singly linked lists and doubly linked lists.

367. **Describe the concepts of "first-fit," "best-fit," and "worst-fit" in memory allocation.**

Answer: These concepts are related to memory allocation in operating systems:

First-Fit: Allocates the first available block of memory that is large enough to satisfy the request.

Best-Fit: Searches for the smallest available block of memory that is large enough to satisfy the request.

Worst-Fit: Allocates the largest available block of memory, which may lead to fragmentation.

These allocation strategies have trade-offs in terms of memory utilization and efficiency.

368. **What is a breadth-first search (BFS) algorithm?**

Answer: Breadth-first search is an algorithm used to traverse or search tree or graph data structures. It explores all neighbor nodes at the present depth before moving to nodes at the next depth level. BFS is often used to find the shortest path in unweighted graphs.

373. **What is the difference between POST and GET HTTP requests?**

Answer: In HTTP, POST and GET are two different request methods used to send data to a server. The main differences are:

GET: Retrieves data from the server and is typically used for read-only operations. Data is included in the URL as query parameters.

POST: Submits data to the server for processing, often used for updates or data creation. Data is included in the request body.

374. **What is the Document Object Model (DOM) in web development?**

Answer: The Document Object Model (DOM) is a programming interface for web documents. It represents the page so that programs can change the document structure, style, and content. It provides a way for programs to interact with web pages dynamically.

375. **Explain the principles of the SOLID design in object-oriented programming.**

Answer: SOLID is an acronym for a set of five design principles in object-oriented programming:

Single Responsibility Principle (SRP): A class should have only one reason to change.

Open/Closed Principle (OCP): Software entities should be open for extension but closed for modification.

Liskov Substitution Principle (LSP): Subtypes must be substitutable for their base types.

Interface Segregation Principle (ISP): Clients should not be forced to depend on interfaces they do not use.

Dependency Inversion Principle (DIP): High-level modules should not depend on low-level modules; both should depend on abstractions.

These principles promote maintainability, extensibility, and flexibility in software design.

376. **What is method overloading in Java?**

Answer: Method overloading is a feature in Java that allows a class to have multiple methods with the same name but different parameter lists (number or types of parameters). The compiler determines which method to call based on the number and types of arguments passed to it.

377. **Describe the concept of "dependency injection."**

Answer: Dependency injection is a design pattern and technique in which a class receives its dependencies (e.g., other objects or services) from external sources rather than creating them itself. This promotes loose coupling and makes the code more modular, testable, and maintainable.

378. **What is the concept of "loose coupling" in software design?**

Answer: Loose coupling is a design principle that aims to minimize the dependencies between components in a software system. Components should interact with each other through well-defined interfaces or abstractions, rather than being tightly coupled. This makes the system more flexible and easier to maintain.

379. Explain the significance of database normalization.

Answer: Database normalization is the process of structuring a database in such a way that it reduces data redundancy and minimizes the likelihood of data anomalies (e.g., update anomalies). It involves breaking down tables and organizing data to eliminate repetitive information. This improves data integrity and efficiency in a database.

380. What are the differences between SQL and NoSQL databases?

Answer: SQL (Structured Query Language) and NoSQL databases have differences in their data models and use cases:

SQL databases are relational, use structured schemas, and are suitable for complex queries and structured data.

NoSQL databases are non-relational, offer flexible schemas, and are well-suited for handling unstructured or semi-structured data and scalability.

381. What is a RESTful API, and how does it work?

Answer: A RESTful API (Representational State Transfer) is a type of web service that follows a set of architectural principles. It uses standard HTTP methods (GET, POST, PUT, DELETE) for communication and typically returns data in a format like JSON or XML. RESTful APIs are designed to be stateless and provide a uniform interface for interacting with resources.

382. Describe the concept of a software testing plan.

Answer: A software testing plan is a document that outlines the testing approach, objectives, scope, resources, and schedule for a software project. It details the testing strategies, test cases, and methodologies to be used, ensuring that the software is thoroughly tested to meet quality standards.

383. What is regression testing, and why is it important?

Answer: Regression testing is the process of retesting a software application after changes or updates have been made to the code. Its primary purpose is to ensure that new changes do not introduce new defects or break existing functionality. Regression testing helps maintain software quality as the project evolves.

384. Explain the "Black Box" and "White Box" testing techniques.

Answer: Black Box and White Box testing are different approaches to software testing:

Black Box Testing: This technique focuses on testing the software's external behavior without knowledge of its internal code. Testers use input data to observe outputs and verify that the software functions as expected.

White Box Testing: This technique involves testing the software's internal code and logic. Testers examine the code to ensure that it meets specified requirements and that all paths and branches are tested.

385. What is the purpose of a code review in software development?

Answer: A code review is a process in which developers review and evaluate each other's code to ensure its quality, correctness, and adherence to coding standards. Code reviews identify bugs, improve code quality, share knowledge, and promote best practices in development.

386. What is a unit test in programming?

Answer: A unit test is a type of testing that focuses on evaluating the smallest parts of a software application, typically individual functions or methods. Unit tests are designed to verify that these parts of the code work correctly and produce expected results in isolation.

387. What is the role of a product manager in software development?

Answer: A product manager is responsible for defining the vision, strategy, and goals for a software product. They work closely with development teams, stakeholders, and customers to prioritize features, manage the product's roadmap, and ensure that it aligns with the organization's objectives.

388. **Explain the difference between a software product and a software project.**

Answer: A software project is a temporary effort to create a specific software solution with defined goals and constraints. A software product, on the other hand, is the result of one or more projects and represents a marketable and maintainable software solution that serves specific purposes or functions.

389. **What is an XOR gate in digital logic?**

Answer: An XOR gate (exclusive OR gate) is a digital logic gate that produces an output of "1" (true) when an odd number of "1" inputs are present. It returns "0" if the number of "1" inputs is even.

390. **Describe the concept of a virtual machine (VM) in computing.**

Answer: A virtual machine is an emulation of a physical computer that runs an operating system and applications. It allows multiple operating systems to run on a single physical machine, enabling greater resource utilization, isolation, and portability.

391. **What are design patterns, and why are they important in software development?**

Answer: Design patterns are general, reusable solutions to common software design problems. They offer established templates for solving specific design challenges, enhancing code quality, reusability, and maintainability. Using design patterns can speed up development and ensure best practices.

392. What is an anti-pattern in software development?

Answer: An anti-pattern is a common solution or design approach that may appear effective but is counterproductive and results in poor software quality or maintainability. Anti-patterns should be avoided as they can lead to problems in software development.

393. What is the purpose of a burn-down chart in agile development?

Answer: A burn-down chart is a visual representation used in agile development to track the progress of a project. It shows the remaining work (typically in story points or tasks) over time, helping the team monitor and manage project velocity and completion.

394. Explain the "fail-fast" principle in software development.

Answer: The "fail-fast" principle is a software design concept that encourages software to detect and report errors as soon as they occur, rather than allowing them to propagate and potentially cause more significant problems later. It promotes early error detection and easier debugging.

395. What is continuous delivery (CD) in the context of software development?

Answer: Continuous delivery is a software development practice that focuses on delivering software to production or a staging environment automatically and frequently. It emphasizes automation, testing, and collaboration to ensure that code changes are always ready for deployment.

396. **Describe the concept of "technical debt" in software development.**

Answer: Technical debt refers to the backlog of incomplete, suboptimal, or hastily implemented code and design decisions in a software project. It represents the trade-off between delivering software quickly and accumulating work for future refactoring and improvement.

397. **What is an API endpoint in web development?**

Answer: An API endpoint is a specific URL or URI (Uniform Resource Identifier) that an API (Application Programming Interface) exposes to allow external systems to interact with it. Each endpoint corresponds to a particular function or resource provided by the API.

398. **Explain the purpose of a "try-catch" block in exception handling.**

Answer: In exception handling, a "try-catch" block is used to enclose code that might raise exceptions. If an exception occurs within the "try" block, it is caught and handled by the corresponding "catch" block. This prevents the program from crashing and allows for graceful error handling.

399. What is a deadlock in multithreading?

Answer: A deadlock is a situation in multithreading or multiprocessing where two or more threads or processes are unable to proceed because each is waiting for the other to release a resource or perform a specific action. This results in a standstill, and the program cannot make progress.

400. Describe the concept of a "race condition" in multithreading.

Answer: A race condition is a concurrency issue that occurs when multiple threads or processes access shared resources or variables concurrently, leading to unpredictable and unintended behavior. The outcome depends on the relative timing and interleaving of operations, which can result in errors.

401. What is a semaphore in operating systems?

Answer: A semaphore is a synchronization mechanism used in operating systems and concurrent programming to control access to shared resources. It helps prevent race conditions by allowing or blocking access to resources based on a set of rules and permits.

402. Explain the concept of an operating system's "kernel."

Answer: The kernel is the core component of an operating system. It manages system resources, such as memory, CPU, input/output devices, and provides essential services to user programs. It acts as an intermediary between applications and hardware, ensuring secure and efficient resource allocation.

403.   **What is the difference between multi-threading and multi-processing?**

Answer: Multi-threading and multi-processing are approaches to achieving parallelism in computing:

Multi-threading: Involves multiple threads within a single process that share the same memory space and can communicate with each other. Threads are lightweight and well-suited for tasks like handling user interfaces.

Multi-processing: Involves multiple processes, each with its own memory space and separate execution. Processes are better suited for parallel tasks on multi-core processors and offer greater isolation.

404.   **What is a semaphore in operating systems?**

Answer: A semaphore is a synchronization mechanism used in operating systems and concurrent programming to control access to shared resources. It helps prevent race conditions by allowing or blocking access to resources based on a set of rules and permits.

405.   **Explain the concept of a "race condition" in multithreading.**

Answer: A race condition is a concurrency issue that occurs when multiple threads or processes access shared resources or variables concurrently, leading to unpredictable and unintended behavior. The outcome depends on the relative timing and interleaving of operations, which can result in errors.

406. What is a deadlock in multithreading?

Answer: A deadlock is a situation in multithreading or multiprocessing where two or more threads or processes are unable to proceed because each is waiting for the other to release a resource or perform a specific action. This results in a standstill, and the program cannot make progress.

407. Describe the purpose of a "packet" in networking.

Answer: In networking, a packet is a unit of data that is transmitted over a network. Packets contain both the actual data to be transmitted and metadata, including source and destination addresses, as well as information for error checking and reassembly at the receiving end.

408. What is a URI (Uniform Resource Identifier) in web development?

Answer: A URI (Uniform Resource Identifier) is a string of characters used to identify a particular resource, often on the internet. URIs can be in the form of URLs (Uniform Resource Locators) or URNs (Uniform Resource Names) and are used to locate and identify resources like web pages, files, and services.

409. Explain the "Same-Origin Policy" in web security.

Answer: The Same-Origin Policy is a security measure in web browsers that restricts web pages from making requests to a different domain (origin) than the one that served the web page. This policy prevents cross-site scripting (XSS) attacks and data theft by enforcing domain-based security boundaries.

410. What is a session in web development?

Answer: In web development, a session is a way to store and track user-specific data across multiple HTTP requests. Sessions are often used to maintain user authentication, shopping cart contents, and other stateful information.

411. Describe the purpose of a "cookie" in web development.

Answer: A cookie is a small piece of data that a web server sends to a user's web browser. The browser stores the cookie and sends it back with each subsequent request to the same server. Cookies are often used to remember user preferences, maintain login sessions, and track user behavior on websites.

412. What is an HTTP status code?

Answer: An HTTP status code is a three-digit numeric code that is included in an HTTP response to indicate the outcome of a request. Status codes are grouped into classes (e.g., 2xx for success, 4xx for client errors, and 5xx for server errors) and provide information about the request's success or failure.

413. Explain the concept of "caching" in web development.

Answer: Caching is the process of storing copies of frequently accessed data in a location that is faster to access than the original source. In web development, caching can be used to speed up web page loading times by storing assets like images, scripts, or pages in the browser or on a proxy server.

414. **What is URL encoding in web development?**

Answer: URL encoding is the process of converting special characters and spaces in a URL into a format that can be transmitted safely over the internet. Special characters are replaced with "%" followed by their ASCII hexadecimal representation. For example, spaces are encoded as "%20."

415. **Explain the concept of a "web server."**

Answer: A web server is software or hardware that serves web content to clients (typically web browsers) over the internet. It processes incoming HTTP requests and delivers web pages, images, documents, or other resources to users. Common web server software includes Apache, Nginx, and Microsoft IIS.

416. **What is the purpose of an "index" in a database?**

Answer: An index in a database is a data structure that improves the speed of data retrieval operations on a database table. It provides a quick way to look up rows based on the values in one or more columns, reducing the need for a full table scan.

417. **Explain the concept of a "stored procedure" in databases.**

Answer: A stored procedure is a precompiled and reusable database program that can be called and executed from within a database management system (DBMS). It typically contains SQL statements and can accept parameters, making it useful for common database tasks and logic.

418. What is a data warehouse in database management?

Answer: A data warehouse is a central repository that aggregates and stores data from various sources for analysis and reporting. It is designed to support business intelligence and data analytics by providing a structured and historical view of data.

419. What is a distributed database system?

Answer: A distributed database system is a database that is spread across multiple physical or logical locations. Data is distributed to improve availability, scalability, and fault tolerance. Each site in the system can access and manipulate data, and changes are often synchronized between sites.

420. Explain the "ACID" properties in database management.

Answer: ACID is an acronym that stands for four key properties of database transactions:

Atomicity: Transactions are atomic and are either fully completed or fully rolled back in case of failure.

Consistency: Transactions bring the database from one consistent state to another.

Isolation: Transactions are isolated from each other, and their operations do not interfere.

Durability: Once a transaction is committed, its changes are permanent and survive system failures.

These properties ensure the reliability and integrity of database transactions.

421. What is CAP theorem in distributed computing?

Answer: The CAP theorem, also known as Brewer's theorem, states that in a distributed computing system, it is impossible to simultaneously guarantee all three of the following:

422. Consistency: All nodes see the same data at the same time.

Availability: Every request receives a response, without guarantee of the data being the latest.

Partition tolerance: The system continues to operate in the presence of network partitions or communication failures.

Distributed databases must make trade-offs between these three properties.

423. What is the "Dark Web," and how does it differ from the "Deep Web"?

Answer: The Dark Web is a part of the internet that is intentionally hidden and inaccessible through standard web browsers. It is often associated with illegal activities and anonymity. In contrast, the Deep Web refers to web content not indexed by search engines and includes legitimate but unindexed pages, such as private databases, intranets, and password-protected sites.

424. Explain the concept of "cybersecurity."

Answer: Cybersecurity is the practice of protecting computer systems, networks, and data from theft, damage, or unauthorized access. It involves implementing measures, technologies, and policies to safeguard information and ensure the confidentiality, integrity, and availability of digital assets.

425. **Describe the concept of "encryption" in data security.**

Answer: Encryption is the process of converting data into a secret code or cipher to protect it from unauthorized access. It ensures that only authorized parties can access and interpret the data, even if it is intercepted by unauthorized entities.

426. **What is a "Denial of Service" (DoS) attack in cybersecurity?**

Answer: A Denial of Service (DoS) attack is a cyberattack that aims to make a network, service, or website unavailable to users by overwhelming it with a flood of traffic or requests. This can result in service disruptions or unavailability for legitimate users.

427. **What is a "Man-in-the-Middle" (MitM) attack in cybersecurity?**

Answer: A Man-in-the-Middle (MitM) attack is a cyberattack in which an attacker intercepts and possibly alters communications between two parties without their knowledge. The attacker can eavesdrop on the communication, modify data, or impersonate one of the parties, posing a significant security threat.

428.   **Explain the concept of a "public key infrastructure" (PKI) in cybersecurity.**

Answer: A public key infrastructure (PKI) is a system of hardware, software, policies, and standards used to manage digital keys and certificates. It provides security services like authentication, data encryption, and digital signatures, enabling secure communication and digital identity verification.

429.   **What is a "virus" in the context of computer security?**

Answer: A virus is a type of malicious software (malware) that attaches itself to legitimate programs or files and spreads to other programs or files when executed. Viruses can damage data, steal information, and compromise the security of a computer system.

430.   **Explain the concept of a "zero-day vulnerability" in cybersecurity.**

Answer: A zero-day vulnerability is a security flaw in software, hardware, or a network that is exploited by attackers before the responsible party has had a chance to fix it or even become aware of it. The term "zero-day" refers to the fact that the flaw is exploited on the same day it is discovered.

431.   **What is "two-factor authentication" (2FA) in cybersecurity?**

Answer: Two-factor authentication (2FA) is a security process that requires users to provide two different authentication factors to gain access to a system or account. The factors typically include something the user knows (e.g., a password) and something the user has (e.g., a smartphone for receiving a temporary code).

432.   What is "ransomware" in the context of cybersecurity?

Answer: Ransomware is a type of malicious software (malware) that encrypts a victim's data or files and demands a ransom for the decryption key. It is a form of extortion, and paying the ransom is discouraged, as it does not guarantee the recovery of data.

433.   What is the "Principle of Least Privilege" in cybersecurity?

Answer: The Principle of Least Privilege (PoLP) is a security principle that dictates that individuals or systems should have the minimum level of access or permissions necessary to perform their tasks. This minimizes the potential for unauthorized access or abuse of privileges.

434.   Explain the concept of a "honeypot" in cybersecurity.

Answer: A honeypot is a security mechanism or system that is intentionally set up to attract and deceive attackers. It is used to monitor and study cyber threats, as well as to divert and distract attackers from real targets, safeguarding critical systems.

435.   What is a "virtual private network" (VPN) in cybersecurity?

Answer: A virtual private network (VPN) is a technology that creates a secure, encrypted connection between a user's device and a remote server or network. It is often used to protect data and privacy when accessing the internet, especially on public networks.

436.   What is the "OWASP Top Ten" in web application security?

Answer: The OWASP Top Ten is a regularly updated list of the ten most critical web application security risks. It is maintained by the Open Web Application Security Project (OWASP) and serves as a guide for identifying and addressing common vulnerabilities in web applications.

437.   Explain the concept of "penetration testing" in cybersecurity.

Answer: Penetration testing, often referred to as "pen testing," is a security assessment method in which ethical hackers simulate real-world cyberattacks to identify vulnerabilities and weaknesses in an organization's systems, networks, and applications. The goal is to strengthen security defenses and protect against real threats.

438.   What is "security by design" in software development and cybersecurity?

Answer: Security by design is an approach to software and system development that emphasizes integrating security practices and considerations from the very beginning of the design and development process. It aims to proactively identify and address security issues, reducing the risk of vulnerabilities and attacks.

439.   What is "blockchain" technology, and how does it work?

Answer: Blockchain is a distributed ledger technology that records transactions across multiple computers in a way that is secure, transparent, and tamper-resistant. It relies on cryptographic techniques and consensus algorithms to validate and store data in a chain of blocks, making it suitable for applications like cryptocurrencies and secure data sharing.

440. **Explain the concept of "smart contracts" in blockchain technology.**

Answer: Smart contracts are self-executing contracts with the terms of the agreement between buyer and seller written directly into code. These contracts run on blockchain platforms and automatically execute and enforce the terms when predefined conditions are met, without the need for intermediaries.

441. **What is "self-driving car" technology?**

Answer: Self-driving car technology, also known as autonomous vehicles, enables cars to navigate and operate without human intervention.

442. **What are "neural networks" in machine learning?**

Answer: Neural networks are computational models inspired by the human brain, used in deep learning for tasks like image recognition and natural language processing.

443. **What is "underfitting" in machine learning?**

Answer: Underfitting occurs when a machine learning model is too simple to capture the underlying patterns in the data, resulting in poor performance on both training and test data.

444. **What is "variance" in machine learning models?**

Answer: Variance in machine learning models is the sensitivity to fluctuations in the training data, leading to a model that fits noise rather than the true pattern.

467. **What is "functional programming"?**

Answer: Functional programming is a programming paradigm that treats computation as the evaluation of mathematical functions and avoids changing state and mutable data.

468. **What is a "closure" in JavaScript?**

Answer: A closure is a function that retains access to variables from its containing (enclosing) function's scope, even after the outer function has finished executing.

469. **What is "asynchronous programming" in JavaScript?**

Answer: Asynchronous programming in JavaScript involves executing tasks without blocking the main program's flow, often used for tasks like fetching data from servers.

470. **What is "dependency injection" in software design?**

Answer: Dependency injection is a design pattern in which dependencies are injected into a class or component rather than being created or managed within it.

471. **What is a "package manager" in software development?**

Answer: A package manager is a tool that automates the process of installing, updating, configuring, and managing software libraries and dependencies.

472. **What is "test-driven development" (TDD) in software development?**

Answer: Test-driven development is a development approach where tests are written before the code, guiding the implementation to ensure that it meets specific requirements.

473. **What is a "REST API" in web development?**

Answer: A REST API (Representational State Transfer Application Programming Interface) is an architectural style for designing networked applications that use HTTP requests to perform CRUD (Create, Read, Update, Delete) operations.

474. **What is "SOAP" in web services?**

Answer: SOAP (Simple Object Access Protocol) is a protocol for exchanging structured information in the implementation of web services.

475. **What is "microservices architecture" in software development?**

Answer: Microservices architecture is an approach to building software systems as a collection of small, independently deployable services that work together.

476. **What is "web scraping," and what are its applications?**

Answer: Web scraping is the process of extracting data from websites. It has applications in data analysis, price comparison, and content aggregation.

477. **What are "websockets" in web development?**

Answer: Websockets provide full-duplex communication channels over a single TCP connection, enabling real-time, two-way communication between a client and server.

478. **What are "authentication" and "authorization" in web security?**

Answer: Authentication verifies a user's identity, while authorization determines the actions and resources a user is allowed to access.

479. **What is "end-to-end encryption" in messaging apps?**

Answer: End-to-end encryption ensures that only the sender and recipient of a message can read its contents, making it highly secure and private.

480. What is "agile software development" and its principles?

Answer: Agile software development is an iterative and flexible approach that prioritizes customer collaboration, responding to change, and delivering working software.

481. What is "machine learning" and its applications?

Answer: Machine learning is a subset of AI that involves training algorithms to make predictions or decisions based on data. It has applications in image recognition, recommendation systems, and more.

482. What is "natural language processing" (NLP) in AI?

Answer: Natural language processing is a field of AI that focuses on the interaction between computers and human language, enabling machines to understand, interpret, and generate human language.

483. What are "Chatbots" and how do they work?

Answer: Chatbots are AI-powered programs that interact with users through text or voice. They use natural language processing to understand and respond to user queries and can be used for customer support and more.

484. What is "machine learning model deployment"?

Answer: Model deployment is the process of making a trained machine learning model available for use in production applications, allowing it to make predictions on new data.

485. What is "model explainability" in machine learning?

Answer: Model explainability refers to the ability to understand and interpret how a machine learning model arrives at its predictions, critical for building trust and meeting regulatory requirements.

486. What is "reinforcement learning" in AI?

Answer: Reinforcement learning is a machine learning paradigm where an agent learns to make decisions by taking actions in an environment to maximize a reward signal.

487. **What is "bias" in machine learning models, and why is it important to address?**

Answer: Bias in machine learning models occurs when the model's predictions are systematically skewed. Addressing bias is crucial to ensure fairness and avoid discrimination.

488. **What is "overfitting" in machine learning, and how can it be prevented?**

Answer: Overfitting occurs when a machine learning model learns the training data too well, but fails to generalize to new, unseen data. It can be prevented by using techniques like regularization and cross-validation.

489. **What are "chatbots" and their use in customer support?**

Answer: Chatbots are AI-driven applications that provide instant responses to customer queries, improving response times and availability in customer support.

490. **What are "knowledge graphs" and how are they used in AI?**

Answer: Knowledge graphs organize and connect information in a structured format, enabling AI systems to understand relationships between entities, which is valuable for natural language understanding and question answering.

491. **What is " Robotic Process Automation " (RPA) and its benefits?**

Answer: RPA is the use of software robots or "bots" to automate repetitive and rule-based tasks, improving efficiency and reducing human error in business processes.

492. What are "no-code" and "low-code" development platforms?

Answer: No-code and low-code platforms enable users to create software applications with minimal or no coding, democratizing app development and making it accessible to non-developers.

493. What is the use of OpenCV in programming?

Answer: OpenCV is an open-source computer vision library that provides tools for image and video analysis, making it valuable for tasks like image processing, object detection, and facial recognition.

494. Why is PyTorch significant in deep learning?

Answer: PyTorch is a popular deep learning framework that offers dynamic computation graphs and strong support for neural networks. It's favored by researchers and developers for its flexibility and ease of use.

495. What is TensorFlow, and how is it used in machine learning?

Answer: TensorFlow is an open-source machine learning framework developed by Google. It's widely used for building and training deep neural networks and other machine learning models.

496. How does NumPy enhance Python for numerical computing?

Answer: NumPy is a library that adds support for large, multi-dimensional arrays and matrices, along with a collection of mathematical functions to Python, making it a foundation for numerical computing.

497. What is the purpose of the Pandas library in Python?

Answer: Pandas is a library for data manipulation and analysis. It provides data structures like DataFrames and Series, making it ideal for handling structured data and time series.

498. How does Matplotlib contribute to data visualization in Python?

Answer: Matplotlib is a popular data visualization library in Python. It enables the creation of various types of plots and charts to visually represent data.

499. What is Scikit-Learn, and how is it used in machine learning?

Answer: Scikit-Learn is a machine learning library for Python that provides tools for classification, regression, clustering, and more. It's widely used for building and evaluating machine learning models.

500. Why is Git a valuable tool for version control in software development?

Answer: Git is a distributed version control system that allows developers to track changes, collaborate on projects, and manage code versions, making it an essential tool for software development.

501. **What is the role of Docker in containerization and deployment?**

Answer: Docker is a platform for developing, shipping, and running applications within containers, ensuring consistency and portability across different environments.

502. **How does Kubernetes help manage containerized applications in a cluster?**

Answer: Kubernetes is an open-source container orchestration system that automates the deployment, scaling, and management of containerized applications in a cluster.

503. **What is the purpose of Flask in web development with Python?**

Answer: Flask is a lightweight Python web framework used to build web applications. It provides essential features for routing, request handling, and template rendering.

504. **How does Node.js differ from traditional server-side languages in web development?**

Answer: Node.js is a runtime environment for executing JavaScript on the server, providing event-driven, non-blocking I/O, and efficient handling of concurrent connections.

505. **What are the advantages of using Spring Framework in Java development?**

Answer: Spring is a Java framework that simplifies the development of enterprise applications by offering features like dependency injection, aspect-oriented programming, and support for various modules.

506. **How does Ruby on Rails simplify web application development?**

Answer: Ruby on Rails, often called Rails, is a web application framework that follows the Model-View-Controller (MVC) architecture, promoting rapid development and convention over configuration.

507. **What is the role of Express.js in building web applications using Node.js?**

Answer: Express.js is a minimal and flexible Node.js web application framework that simplifies the creation of web and mobile applications.

508. **Why is Django a popular framework for Python web development?**

Answer: Django is a high-level Python web framework that encourages rapid development, clean, pragmatic design, and follows the Model-View-Controller (MVC) architectural pattern.

www.ingramcontent.com/pod-product-compliance
Lightning Source LLC
LaVergne TN
LVHW051713050326
832903LV00032B/4188